To a very dear friend.
I hope that our friendship
can remain always the
way it is today.
Happy Birthday
Love,
Annie

FRIENDS TOGETHER

FRIENDS

TOGETHER

Beautiful Writings
About the Gift of Friendship

HALLMARK CROWN EDITIONS

FRIENDS TOGETHER

What Is a Friend?

A friend is a person of great understanding
Who shares all our hopes and our schemes,
A companion who listens with infinite patience
To all of our plans and our dreams,
A true friend can make all our cares melt away
With the touch of a hand or a smile,
And with calm reassurance make everything brighter,
And life always seem more worthwhile—
A friend shares so many bright moments of laughter
At even the tiniest thing—
What memorable hours of light-hearted gladness
And pleasure this sharing can bring!
A friend is a cherished and precious possession
Who knows all our hopes and our fears,
And someone to treasure deep down in our hearts
With a closeness that grows through the years!
            Katherine Davis

Life is nothing without friendship.   *Cicero*

Old Friendships Are the Dearest

Though many of life's pleasures
May change from year to year,
Old friendships never change at all
Except to grow more dear,
And just like cherished memories,
They have a place apart—
A place reserved forever
In a corner of the heart.

Barbara Burrow

Joy in Life

It is my joy in life to find
At every turning of the road
The strong arms of a comrade kind
To help me onward with my load;
And since I have no gold to give,
And love alone must make amends,
My only prayer is, while I live—
God make me worthy of my friends.

F. D. Sherman

Give Me One Friend

Give me one friend, just one, who meets
The needs of all my varying moods;
Be we in noisy city street,
Or in dear Nature's solitudes.

One who can let the World go by,
And suffer not a minute's pang;
Who'd dare to shock propriety
With me, and never care a hang.

One who can share my grief or mirth,
And know my days to praise or curse;
And rate me just for what I'm worth,
And find me still,—Oh, not so worse!

Give me one friend, for peace or war,
And I shall hold myself well blest,
And richly compensated for
The cussedness of all the rest.

Esther M. Clark

The Art of Friendship

The first step in the art of friendship is to be a friend; then making friends takes care of itself. To be a friend a man should start by being a friend to himself, by being true to his highest and best and by aligning himself with the enduring values of human life that make for growth and progress.

To be a friend a man should strive to be "like the shadow of a great rock in a weary land," to be a source of refuge and strength to those who walk in darkness.

To be a friend a man should believe in the inherent goodness of men and in their potential greatness; he should treat men in a big spirit, expectant of a noble response.

To be a friend a man should strive to lift people up, not cast them down; to encourage, not discourage; to set an example that will be an inspiration to others.

To be a friend a man should be sensitively responsive to the dreams and aims of others and should show sincere appreciation for the contributions others make to the enrichment of his life.

To be a friend a man should practice the companionship of silence and the magic of words that his speech may build and not destroy, help and not hinder.

To be a friend a man should close his eyes to the faults of others and open them to his own.

To be a friend a man should not attempt to reform or reprimand, but should strive only to make others happy if he can.

To be a friend a man should be himself, he should be done with hypocrisy, artificiality and pretense, he should meet and mingle with people in quiet simplicity and humility.

To be a friend a man should be tolerant, he should have an

understanding heart and a forgiving nature, knowing that all men stumble now and then, and that he who never made a mistake never accomplished anything.

To be a friend a man should join hands with all people who are working for great principles, great purposes and great causes; he should put his shoulder to the wheel to help achieve common goals.

To be a friend a man should go more than halfway with his fellow men; he should greet others first and not wait to be greeted; he should radiate a spirit of overflowing good will.

To be a friend a man should remember that we are human magnets; that like attracts like, and that what we give we get.

To be a friend a man should recognize that no man knows all the answers, and that he should add each day to his knowledge of how to live the friendly way.

Wilferd A. Peterson

My House of Friendship

I built a house of friendship through the years
Each block a kindly thought is held in place
By mortar made of tenderness and tears
For others' woes. The rooms are large with space
For all my friends. There is not strain nor stress.
Foundation stones are love and loyalty,
And over all a roof of cheerfulness.
Mirrored upon the walls where we may see,
Are memories, some etched in brilliant hue
While some are dark; and down the corridors
Come echoes of glad voices old and new;
Times when my spirit droops or when it soars,
I find response here where my travels end
The house that you have helped to build, my friend!

Alma Jeffries Stull

The comfort of having a friend may be taken away,
but not that of having had one.   *Seneca*

A Friend Sees the Best In Us

Once in an age, God sends to some of us a friend who loves in us, not a false-imagining, an unreal character, but, looking through the rubbish of our imperfections, loves in us the divine ideal of our nature,—loves, not the man that we are, but the angel that we may be.   *Harriet Beecher Stowe*

Truthfulness

Every friendship that lasts is built of certain durable materials. The first of these is truthfulness. If I cannot look into the eyes of my friend and speak out always the truthful thought and feeling with the simplicity of a little child, there can be no real friendship between us. Friends who have to be "handled" or "managed," or with whom we take refuge in fencing or posing, do not know the love that casts out fear. "Trust is the first requisite for making a friend," says Hugh Black,—"faithfulness is the first requisite for keeping him"; and trust and faithfulness cannot endure without truthfulness.

Bertha Conde

Mutual Affection

Nature produced us related to one another, since she created us from the same source and to the same end. She engendered in us mutual affection and made us prone to friendships. . . . Through her orders, our hands are ready to help in the good work. Our relations with one another are like a stone arch, which would collapse if the stones did not mutually support each other, and which is upheld in this very way.

Seneca

No Rival

Common friendships will admit of division; one may love the beauty of this, the good humor of that person, the liberality of a third, the paternal affection of a fourth, the fraternal love of a fifth, and so on. But this friendship that possesses the whole soul, and there rules and sways with an absolute sovereignty, can admit of no rival.

Michel Eyquem Montaigne

Old Coats, Old Friends

My coat and I live comfortably together. It has assumed all my wrinkles, does not hurt me anywhere, has moulded itself on my deformities, and is complacent to all my movements, and I only feel its presence because it keeps me warm. Old coats and old friends are the same thing.

Victor Hugo

All Losses Restored

When to the sessions of sweet silent thought
I summon up remembrance of things past,
I sigh the lack of many a thing I sought,
And with old woes new wail my dear time's waste :
Then can I drown an eye, unused to flow,
For precious friends hid in death's dateless night,
And weep afresh love's long since cancelled woe,
And moan the expense of many a vanished sight :
Then can I grieve at grievances foregone,
And heavily from woe to woe tell o'er
The sad account of fore-bemoaned moan,
Which I new pay as if not paid before.
But if the while I think on thee, dear friend,
All losses are restored and sorrows end.

Shakespeare

Make not thy friend too cheap to thee,
nor thyself too dear to him.

James Howell

Woman as Friend

It is a wonderful advantage to a man, in every pursuit or avocation, to secure an adviser in a sensible woman. In woman there is at once a subtle delicacy of tact, and a plain soundness of judgment, which are rarely combined to an equal degree in man.

A woman, if she be really your friend, will have a sensitive regard for your character, honor, repute. She will seldom counsel you to do a shabby thing; for a woman friend always desires to be proud of you. At the same time, her constitutional timidity makes her more cautious than your male friend. She, therefore, seldom counsels you to do an imprudent thing. By friendships, I mean pure friendships—those in which there is no admixture of the passion of love, except in the married state.

A man's best female friend is a wife of good sense and good heart, whom he loves, and who loves him. If he have that, he need not seek elsewhere. *Sir Edward Bulwer-Lytton*

To make the world a friendly place
One must show it a friendly face.
James Whitcomb Riley

The Substance of Life

This matter of friendship is often regarded slightingly as a mere accessory of life, a happy chance if one falls into it, but not as entering into the substance of life. No mistake can be greater. It is, as Emerson says, not a thing of "glass threads or frost-work, but the solidest thing we know."

T. T. Munger

I don't meddle with what my friends believe or reject, any more than I ask whether they are rich or poor; I love them.

James Russell Lowell

The Love of Friendship

The love of friendship should be gratuitous. You ought not to have or to love a friend for what he will give you. If you love him for the reason that he will supply you with money or some other temporal favor, you love the gift rather than him. A friend should be loved freely for himself, and not for anything else.

St. Augustine

Daily Creed

Let me be a little kinder,
Let me be a little blinder
To the faults of those about me,
Let me praise a little more.

Let me be, when I am weary,
Just a little bit more cheery;
Let me serve a little better
The God we would adore.

Let me be a little meeker
With the brother who is weaker;
Let me strive a little harder
To be all that I should be.

Let me be more understanding,
And a little less demanding,
Let me be the sort of friend
That you have always been to me.

John Grey

To Be a Friend

In India 2500 years ago, a man named Gautama Buddha walked the roads and preached and taught. His teachings are still remembered by five hundred million Buddhist believers in Asia and the Orient.

I am not a Buddhist. But I find no disloyalty to my faith in accepting advice as practical today as it was when Buddha first offered it. In a mango grove in Bihar he told one of his disciples that five things are necessary to achieve release from unhappiness and fear. These, he said, include: restraint, proper discourse, energy in producing good thoughts, firmness in pursuing them, and acquisition of true insight. But first of all, and above all, he said, the seeker must learn to be a good friend.

When people asked for a definition of friendliness, Buddha answered, "It means to have hope of the welfare of others more than for one's self. . . . It means affection unsullied by hope or thought of any reward on earth or in heaven."

Buddha admitted that such generous wholeheartedness would not be easy. Yet in the long run it is intensely practical. "Compassion and knowledge and virtue," he said, "are the only possessions that do not fade away."

"To be a good friend...." How simple it sounds—just five short words. Yet how much they represent! Think how much it could mean, a flowing out of new forces of friendship from person to person, and eventually from land to land.

Try as we may, there is no other form of security. As Buddha said, "Friendship is the only cure for hatred, the only guarantee of peace."   *Robert Hardy Andrews*

Small Service

Small service is true service while it lasts;
Of friends, however humble, scorn not one;
The daisy, by the shadow that it casts,
Protects the lingering dewdrop from the sun.
William Wordsworth

Interest in People

You can make more friends in two months by becoming really interested in other people, than you can in two years by trying to get other people interested in you. Which is just another way of saying that the way to make a friend is to be one.

Dale Carnegie

Friendship cheers like a sunbeam; charms like a good story; inspires like a brave leader; binds like a golden chain; guides like a heavenly vision. *Newell D. Hillis*

A true test of friendship,—to sit or walk with a friend for an hour in perfect silence without wearying of one another's company.

Dinah Mulock Craik

The Warmth of Friendship

As you say, we don't need soft skies to make friendship a joy to us. What a heavenly thing it is; "World without end," truly. I grow warm thinking of it, and should glow at the thought if all the glaciers of the Alps were heaped over me! Such friends God has given me in this little life of mine!

Celia Thaxter

It is well that there is no one without a fault, for he would not have a friend in the world.

William Hazlitt

If thou findest a good man, rise up early in the morning to go to him, and let thy feet wear the steps of his door.

The Apocryphal Book of Ecclesiasticus

Thank You, Friend

I never came to you, my friend,
And went away without
Some new enrichment of the heart:
More faith, and less of doubt,
More courage for the days ahead,
And often in great need
Coming to you, I went away
Comforted, indeed.

How can I find the shining words,
The glowing phrase that tells
All that your love has meant to me,
All that your friendship spells?
There is no word, no phrase for you
On whom I so depend,
All I can say to you is this:
God bless you, precious friend.

Grace Noll Crowell

What a thing friendship is—
World without end!

Robert Browning

Three Friendships

There are three friendships which are advantageous, and three which are injurious. Friendship with the upright; friendship with the sincere; and friendship with the man of much observation; these are advantageous. Friendship with the man of specious airs; friendship with the insinuatingly soft; and friendship with the glib-tongued; these are injurious. *Confucius*

Friends Improve With Age

Time draweth wrinkles in a fair face, but addeth fresh colors to a fast friend, which neither heat, nor cold, nor misery, nor place, nor destiny, can alter or diminish. *John Lyly*

One-of-a-Kind

We can never replace a friend. When a man is fortunate enough to have several, he finds they are all different. No one has a double in friendship. *Friedrich von Schiller*

He that ceaseth to be a friend never was a good one. *H. G. Bohn*

Friendship

Friendship is the allay of our sorrows, the ease of our passions, the discharge of our oppressions, the sanctuary to our calamities, the counsellor of our thoughts, the exercise and improvement of what we meditate.   *Jeremy Taylor*

Friends Soothe the Spirit

We do not wish for friends to feed and clothe our bodies—neighbors are kind enough for that—but to do the like office to our spirits. For this, few are rich enough, however well disposed they may be.   *Henry David Thoreau*

When a friend asks, there is no tomorrow.   *George Herbert*

A Friend Listens

I have noted that the best and closest friends are those who seldom call on each other for help. In fact, such is almost the finest definition of a friend—a person who does not need us but who is able to enjoy us.

I have seldom suffered over the troubles of a friend. Are his mishaps short of tragedy, I am inclined to chuckle. And he is seldom serious in telling me of his misfortunes. He makes anecdotes out of them, postures comically in their midst and tries to entertain me with them. This is one of the chief values of my friendship, as it is of his. We enable each other to play the strong man superior to his fate. Given a friend to listen, my own disasters change color. I win victories while relating them. Not only have I a friend on my side who will believe my version of the battle—and permit me to seem a victor in my communiqués—but I have actually a victory in me. I am able to show my friend my untouched side. My secret superiority to bad events becomes stronger when I can speak and have a friend believe in it.

Ben Hecht

Friendship maketh daylight in the understanding, out of darkness and confusion of thoughts.

Francis Bacon

The Rarest Faith

Friendship takes place between those who have an affinity for one another, and is a perfectly natural and inevitable result. No professions or advances will avail. Even speech, at first, necessarily has nothing to do with it; but it follows after silence, as the buds in the graft do not put forth into leaves till long after the graft has taken. It is a drama in which the parties have no part to act. . . .

Friendship is never established as an understood relation. Do you demand that I be less your friend that you may know it? Yet what right have I to think that another cherishes so rare a sentiment for me? It is a miracle which requires constant proofs. It is an exercise of the finest imagination and the rarest faith. It says by a silent but eloquent behavior: "I will be so related to thee as thou canst not imagine; even so thou mayest believe. I will spend truth, all my wealth on thee," and the friend responds silently through his nature, and life, and treats his friend with the same divine courtesy. . . .

The language of Friendship is not words but meaning. It is an intelligence above language. One imagines endless conversations with his friend, in which the tongue shall be loosed, and thoughts be spoken, without hesitancy, or end; but the experience is commonly far otherwise. . . .

Suppose you go to bid farewell to your friend who is setting out on a journey; what other outward sign do you know than to shake his hand . . . ? There are some things which a man never speaks of, which are much finer kept silent about. To the highest communications we only lend a silent ear. . . . In human intercourse the tragedy begins, not when there is misunderstanding about words, but when silence is not understood.

Henry David Thoreau

Our Friendship

Our friendship
Is like white sails
On a slow-moving sea
Against sunny blue
And fluffs of shining clouds.

It is slender poplars
Swaying by the lake,
Reaching up to silver stars
Paled by radiant moonbeams.

It is cool, slow rain
On an April day,
Lulling a weary brain
To peace and quiet.

Helen Dirks

The Freedom of Friendship

A man cannot speak to his son but as a father, to his wife but as a husband, to his enemy but upon terms; whereas a friend may speak as the case requires, and not as it sorteth with the person.

Francis Bacon

Always a Friend

A true friend unbosoms freely, advises justly, assists readily, adventures boldly, takes all patiently, defends courageously, and continues a friend unchangeably. In short, choose a friend as thou dost a wife, till death separate you. Death cannot kill what never dies. Nor can spirits ever be divided that love and live in the same Divine Principle. This is the comfort of friends, that though they may be said to die, yet their friendship and society are, in the best sense, ever present, because immortal.   *William Penn*

Sharing

If a man could mount to Heaven and survey the mighty universe, his admiration of its beauties would be much diminished unless he had someone to share in his pleasure.   *Cicero*

Elmwood, February 27, 1867

My Dear Longfellow,

—On looking back, I find that our personal intercourse is now nearly thirty years' date. It began on your part in a note acknowledging my Class Poem much more kindly than it deserved. Since then it has ripened into friendship, and there has never been a jar between us. If there had been, it would certainly have been my fault and not yours. Friendship is called the wine of life, and there certainly is a stimulus in it that warms and inspires as we grow older. Ours should have some body to have kept so long. . . .

I remain always affectionately yours,

JRL
[James Russell Lowell]

Friendship's Growth

Friendships do not grow up in any carefully tended and contemplated fashion. . . . They begin haphazard.

As we look back on the first time we saw our friends we find that generally our original impression was curiously astray. We have worked along beside them, have consorted with them drunk or sober, have grown to cherish their delicious absurdities, have outrageously imposed on each other's patience—and suddenly we awoke to realize what had happened.

We had, without knowing it, gained a new friend. In some curious way the unseen border line had been passed. We had reached the final culmination of Anglo-Saxon regard when two men rarely look each other straight in the eyes because they are ashamed to show each other how fond they are.

We had reached the fine flower and the ultimate test of comradeship—that is, when you get a letter from one of your best friends, you know you don't need to answer it until you get ready to.   *Christopher Morley*

The Ways of Friendship

Let thy pity be a divining: to know first if thy friend wanteth pity. Perhaps he loveth in thee the unmoved eye, and the look of eternity.

Let thy pity for thy friend be hid under a hard shell; thou shalt bite out a tooth upon it. Thus will it have delicacy and sweetness.

Art thou pure air and solitude and bread and medicine to thy friend? Many a one cannot loosen his own fetters, but is nevertheless his friend's emancipator.

Art thou a slave? Then thou canst not be a friend. Art thou a tyrant? Then thou canst not have friends.

Friedrich Nietzsche

Tell Him Now

If you have a friend worth loving,
Love him, yes, and let him know
That you love him ere life's evening
Tinge his brow with sunset glow;
Why should good words ne'er be said
Of a friend till he is dead?
Thomas Hughes

Friendship that flows from the heart
    cannot be frozen by adversity,
      as the water that flows from the spring
    cannot congeal in winter.
James Fenimore Cooper

Our chief want in life is somebody
    who shall make us do what we can.
This is the service of a friend.
Ralph Waldo Emerson

A Faithful Friend

A faithful friend is a sturdy shelter:
    he that has found one
    has found a treasure.
There is nothing so precious as a
    faithful friend,
and no scales can measure his excellence.
The Apocryphal Book of Ecclesiasticus

Friendship improves happiness,
    and abates misery,
by doubling our joy,
    and dividing our grief.
Joseph Addison

Be slow to fall into friendship;
    but when thou art in,
    continue firm and constant.
Socrates

In Constant Repair

I have often thought that as longevity is generally desired, and I believe generally expected, it would be wise to be continually adding to the number of our friends, that the loss of some may be supplied by others.

Friendship, the wine of life, should be like a well-stocked cellar, be thus continually renewed; and it is consolatory to think, that although we can seldom add what will equal the generous first-growth, yet friendship becomes insensibly old in much less time than is commonly imagined, and not many years are required to make it very mellow and pleasant.

Warmth will, no doubt, make considerable difference. Men of affectionate temper and bright fancy will coalesce a great deal sooner than those who are cold and dull. This [proposition] was the opinion of [Dr. Samuel] Johnson himself. He said to Sir Joshua Reynolds, "If a man does not make new acquaintances through life, he will soon find himself left alone. A man, Sir, should keep his friendships in constant repair." *James Boswell*

Friendship, gift of Heaven, delight of great souls; friendship, which kings, so distinguished for ingratitude, are unhappy enough not to know. *Francois de Voltaire*

False Charges

I hear it was charged against me that I
sought to destroy institutions,
But really I am neither for nor against institutions,
Only I will establish in the Mannahatta
and in every city of these States,
inland and seaboard,
And in the fields and woods, and above
every keel little or large
that dents the water,
The institution of the dear love of comrades.

Walt Whitman

Reward

From quiet homes and first beginning,
Out to the undiscovered ends,
There's nothing worth the wear of winning
But laughter and the love of friends.

Hilaire Belloc

Precious Friendship

Friendship is a vase, which, when it is flawed by heat or violence
or accident, may as well be broken at once; it can never be trusted
after. The more graceful and ornamental it was, the more clearly
do we discern the hopelessness of restoring it to its former state.
Coarse stones, if they are fractured, may be cemented again; precious ones never.

Walter Savage Landor

O Friend!

O friend, my bosom said,
Through thee alone the sky is arched,
Through thee the rose is red,
All things through thee take nobler form,
And look beyond the earth,
The mill-round of our fate appears
A sun-path in thy worth.
Me, too, thy nobleness has taught
To master my despair;
The fountains of my hidden life
Are through thy friendship fair.

Ralph Waldo Emerson

The Value of Friends

We never know the true value of friends. While they live we are too sensitive of their faults: when we have lost them we only see their virtues.
J. C. and A. W. Hare

The making of friends who are real friends, is the best token we have of a man's success in life.
Edward Everett Hale

Friends Are Not a One-Way Street

Friendships can be infinitely varied.

And by their very differentness the whole pattern of one's days can be enlivened, and in so many ways rewarding.

Sift through your friendships; sort them.

There is the rich inner circle of those people who are dearest to the heart. Usually these are the persons to whom we can most honestly express our deepest selves. And even though we may not see them for days, weeks on end—even years—the bond remains strong and special and true.

Yet would we not be the poorer without the infinite variety of others?

Friends can be friends for so many different reasons.

There is the wonderfully helpful neighbor who is always willing to give you a hand with the children, or whip up a skirt for you.

There is the witty one who can always make you laugh.

There is the one who sends over bones for the dog, and is generous with praise for your growing crew.

There is the quiet soul who occasionally comes up with a startling gem of philosophy.

It takes patience sometimes to appreciate the true value in the people with whom circumstances have surrounded us. It takes awareness to recognize these values when they appear.

Yet almost everyone has something uniquely his own to contribute to our lives—and equally important, a place in his own life that perhaps we alone can satisfy.

The heart has many doors. Don't be too quick to bolt them.

Marjorie Holmes

This Is Friendship

It is one of the severest tests of friendship to tell your friend of his faults. If you are angry with a man, or hate him, it is not hard to go to him and stab him with words; but so to love a man that you cannot bear to see the stain of sin upon him, and to speak painful truth through loving words—this is friendship. But few have such friends. Our enemies usually teach us what we are, at the point of the sword.

Henry Ward Beecher

An Act of Faith

The quality of friendship, unlike that of mercy, is continually being strained. But it is the essence of friendship that it can stand the strain. Friendship is like love at its best: not blind but sympathetically all-seeing; a support which does not wait for understanding; an act of faith which does not need, but always has, reason.

Louis Untermeyer

My Estate

My friends are my estate. Forgive me then the avarice to hoard them! They tell me those who were poor early have different views of gold. I don't understand how that is. God is not so wary as we, else He would give us no friends, lest we forget Him! The charms of the heaven in the bush are superseded, I fear, by the heaven in the hand occasionally.

Emily Dickinson

Autumn Friendships

It is great to have friends when one is young, but indeed it is still more so when you are getting old. When we are young, friends are, like everything else, a matter of course. In the old days we know what it means to have them.

Edward Grieg

How can life be true life without friends?

Ennius

To Our Guest

If you come cheerily,
Here shall be jest for you;
If you come wearily,
Here shall be rest for you.
If you come borrowing,
Gladly we'll loan to you;
If you come sorrowing,
Love shall be shown to you.
Under our thatch, friend,
Place shall abide for you;
Touch but the latch, friend,
The door shall swing wide for you!
Nancy Byrd Turner

No Friend to Spare

He who has a thousand friends,
Has not a friend to spare,
And he who has one enemy
Will meet him everywhere.
Ali Ben Abu Taheb

49

New Friends and Old Friends

Make new friends, but keep the old;
Those are silver, these are gold.
New-made friendships, like new wine,
Age will mellow and refine.
Friendships that have stood the test—
Time and change—are surely best;
Brow may wrinkle, hair grow gray;
Friendship never knows decay.
For 'mid old friends, tried and true,
Once more we our youth renew.
But old friends, alas! may die;
New friends must their place supply.
Cherish friendship in your breast—
New is good, but old is best;
Make new friends, but keep the old;
Those are silver, these are gold.

Joseph Parry

Be a Friend

Vex no man's secret soul—if that can be—
The path of life hath far too many a thorn!
Help whom thou may'st—for surely unto thee
Sharp need of help will e'er the end be borne.
Sa'di

Fair-Weather Friend

That friend who serves, and seeks for gain,
And follows but for form,
Will pack when it begins to rain,
And leave you in the storm.
William Shakespeare

To distrust a friend is a double folly.
Trust *is* friendship.
Bryant A. Wooster

Sacrifices for Friendship

There are people who believe that man's life is a continuous flight from pain and a persistent search for pleasure. I have never seen a human being of whom that is true. It is true only of beings who have lost their humanity, either through complete disintegration or through mental illness.

The ordinary human being is able to sacrifice pleasures and to take pain upon himself for a cause, for somebody or something he loves and deems worthy of pain and sacrifice. He can disregard both pain and pleasure because he is directed not towards his pleasure but towards the things he loves and with which he wants to unite.

If we desire something because of the pleasure we may get out of it, we may get the pleasure but we shall not get joy. If we try to

52

find someone through whom we may get pleasure, we may get pleasure but we shall not have joy. If we search for something in order to avoid pain, we may avoid pain, but we shall not avoid sorrow. If we try to use someone to protect us from pain, he may protect us from pain but he will not protect us from sorrow.

Pleasures can be provided and pain can be avoided, if we use or abuse other beings. But joy cannot be attained and sorrow cannot be overcome in this way. Joy is possible only when we are driven towards things and persons because of what they are and not because of what we can get from them.   *Paul Tillich*

Best Together

Strike hands with me, the glasses brim,
the sun is on the heather
And love is good and life is long
and two are best together.
Edward Wrightman

Riches

We are the weakest of spendthrifts if we let one friend drop off
through inattention, or let one push away another, or if we hold
aloof from one for petty jealousy or heedless roughness. Would
you throw away a diamond because it pricked you? One good
friend is not to be weighed against all the jewels of the earth.

Will Carleton

A Prudent Companion

If a man find a prudent companion who walks with him, is wise,
and lives soberly, he may walk with him, overcoming all danger,
happy, but considerate. *The Buddha*

More Valuable Than Gold

If all the gold in the world were melted down into a solid cube it would be about the size of an eight-room house. If a man got possession of all that gold—billions of dollars worth, he could not buy a friend, character, peace of mind, clear conscience, or a sense of beauty.   *Charles Banning*

Actions Speak Louder

A slender acquaintance with the world must convince every man that actions, not words, are the true criterion of the attachment of friends; and that the most liberal professions of goodwill are very far from being the surest marks of it.   *George Washington*

Words Are Not Enough

We call that person who has lost his father an orphan; and a widower, that man who has lost his wife. And that man who has known that immense unhappiness of losing a friend, by what name do we call him? Here every human language holds its peace in impotence.   *Joseph Rioux*

One of the most beautiful qualities of true friendship
is to understand and to be understood.   *Seneca*

The Arrow and The Song

I shot an arrow into the air,
It fell to earth, I know not where;
For, so swiftly it flew, the sight
Could not follow it in its flight.

I breathed a song into the air,
It fell to earth, I knew not where;
For who has sight so keen and strong,
That it can follow the flight of song?

Long, long afterward, in an oak
I found the arrow, still unbroke;
And the song, from beginning to end,
I found again in the heart of a friend.

Henry Wadsworth Longfellow

Destiny

There is a destiny which makes us brothers,—
None goes on his way alone;
All that we send into the lives of others,
Comes back into our own.

Edwin Markham

The Strength of Friendship

Life is a chronicle of friendship.
Friends create the world anew each day.
Without their loving care,
*   courage would not suffice*
*   to keep hearts strong for life.*
*   Helen Keller*

My Dear Liszt:

I must say, you are a friend. Let me say more to you, for although I always recognized in friendship between men the noblest and highest relation, it was you who embodied this idea into its fullest reality by letting me no longer imagine, but feel and grasp, what a friend is. I do not thank you, for you alone have the power to thank yourself by your joy in being what you are. It is noble to have a friend, but still nobler to be a friend.

Richard Wagner

The Lesson of Friendship

Friendship is an education. It draws the friend out of himself and all that is selfish and ignoble in him and leads him to life's higher levels of altruism and sacrifice. Many a man has been saved from a life of frivolity and emptiness to a career of noble service by finding at a critical hour the right kind of friend.   *G. D. Prentice*

The Habit of Friendship

As widowers proverbially marry again, so a man with the habit of friendship always finds new friends. . . . My old age judges more charitably and thinks better of mankind than my youth ever did. I discount idealization, I forgive onesidedness, I see that it is essential to perfection of any kind. And in each person I catch the fleeting suggestion of something beautiful, and swear eternal friendship with that.   *George Santayana*

Breathing Room

There can be no friendship where there is no freedom. Friendship loves a free air, and will not be penned up in straight and narrow enclosures.   *William Penn*

Friends

Men are so much less demanding in friendship. A woman wants her friends to be perfect. She sets a pattern, usually a reasonable facsimile of herself, lays a friend out on this pattern and worries and prods at any little qualities which do not coincide with her own image. She simply won't be bothered with anything less than ninety per cent congruity, and will accept the ninety per cent only if the other ten per cent is shaping up nicely and promises accurate conformity within a short time. Friends with glaring lumps or un-smoothable rough places are cast off like ill-fitting garments, and even if this means that the woman has no friends at all, she seems happier than with some imperfect being for whom she would have to make allowances.

A man has a friend, period. He acquires this particular friend because they both like to hunt ducks. The fact that the friend discourses entirely in four letter words, very seldom washes, chews tobacco and spits at random, is drunk a good deal of the time and hates women, in no way affects the friendship. If the man notices these flaws in the perfection of his friend, he notices them casually as he does his friend's height, the color of his eyes, the width of his shoulders; and the friendship continues at an even temperature for years and years and years.   *Betty Mac Donald*

Old Friends

There is no friend like the old friend who
    has shared our morning days,
No greeting like his welcome, no homage
    like his praise;
Fame is the scentless sunflower, with
    gaudy crown of gold;
But friendship is the breathing rose,
    with sweets in every fold.

Oliver Wendell Holmes

A Worthy Friendship

The very idea of a worthy friendship implies that the friends need and desire each other; are sure that each has much to give to the other; and so are continuously receptive and eager for the other's gift. Unteachableness shuts one off from his friend's best gift.

Henry Churchill King

A Divine League

Friends are the Ancient and Honorable of the earth. The oldest men did not begin friendship. It is older than Hindustan and the Chinese Empire. How long it has been cultivated, and still it is the staple article! It is a divine league forever struck.

Henry David Thoreau

Give and Take

Without reciprocal mildness and temperance there can be no continuance of friendship. Every man will have something to do for his friend, and something to bear with in him.   *Owen Felltham*

The Warmth of Friendship

And when the wintry tempest blows,
And January's sleets and snows
Are spread o'er every vale and hill,
With one to tell a merry tale
O'er roasted nuts and humming ale,
sit, and care not for the gale;—
And let the world laugh, an' it will.

Luis De Gongora Y Argote

A Gift

Blessed are they who have the gift of making friends, for it is one of God's best gifts. It involves many things, but above all, the power of going out of one's self, and appreciating whatever is noble and loving in another.   *Thomas Hughes*

One Friend

If words came as readily as ideas and ideas as feeling, I could say ten hundred kindly things. You know my supreme happiness at having one on earth whom I can call a friend.   *Charles Lamb*

Richer Friendship

He who would grow into larger and richer friendships must recognize first of all that, if his friend is in truth worthy of such a friendship as he seeks, the great way is by personal association. One cannot grab up and hurry off with the fine fruits of friendship. No friendship that counts for much with either men or God can become one's own without the giving of time, of thought, of attention, of honest response. . . . No friendship is so high, so fine, or so assured that it does not need that the friends should take time to be together, that they should be willing to think enough to enter with some appreciation into the thought and experience of each other, and that they should make honest response to the best in each other's character and in each other's vision.

Henry C. King

Understanding and Trust

The very best thing is good talk, and the thing that helps it most, is *friendship*. How it dissolves the barriers that divide us, and loosens all constraints, and diffuses itself like some fine old cordial through all the veins of life—this feeling that we understand and trust each other, and wish each other heartily well! Everything into which it really comes is good. It transforms letterwriting from a task to a pleasure. It makes music a thousand times more sweet. The people who play and sing not *at us*, but *to us*—how delightful it is to listen to them! Yes, there is a talkability that can express itself even without words. There is an exchange of thoughts and feelings which is happily alike in speech and in silence. It is quietness pervaded with friendship.   *Henry van Dyke*

True Friendship

'Tis hard to find in life
A friend, a bow, a wife,
Strong, supple to endure,
In stock and sinew pure,
In time of danger sure.

False friends are common. Yes, but where
True nature links a friendly pair,
The blessing is as rich as rare.

To bitter ends
You trust true friends,
Not wife nor mother,
Not son nor brother.

No long experience alloys
True friendship's sweet and supple joys;
No evil men can steal the treasure;
'Tis death, death only, sets a measure.

From the Panchatantra

Tell Your Troubles

I was angry with my friend:
I told my wrath, my wrath did end.
I was angry with my foe;
I told it not, my wrath did grow.

William Blake

He Is My Friend!

He is my friend! The words
Brought Summer and the birds;
And all my Winter time
Thawed into running rhyme
And rippled into song,
Warm, tender, brave and strong.

And so it sings to-day—
So may it sing alway!
Let each mute measure end
 With "Still he is my friend."

James Whitcomb Riley

The Quiet Hours

It is good to pause and rest awhile
From life's demanding pace . . .
To leave the loud,
Chaotic crowd
And find a peaceful place,
To put on the cloak of quietness
With heart and mind at ease,
To sit with a friend
At the long day's end
And recall fond memories.
And whether we talk or whether we dream,
You'll find that in the end,
No treasure, though rare,
Could ever compare
With the quiet hours spent with a friend.

Barbara Burrow

As gold more splendid
    from the fire appears,
Thus friendship brightens
    by the length of years.

Thomas Carlyle

The Meaning of Friendship

What does it mean to be a friend?
A helping hand to the journey's end;
A loyal heart and a loving, too,
No task too great for a friend to do!

What does it mean to be a friend?
A tongue that is quickest to defend.
A friend comes through when the test demands;
A friend is a person who understands.

Anne Campbell

Set in Weiss Roman, designed by Emil Rudolf Weiss for the Bauer Typographic Foundry. Typography by Joseph Thuringer and set at the Rochester Typographic Service. Printed on Hallmark Eggshell Book Paper. Designed by Trudi M. Boese